Alien In My Pocket

Cosmic Characters for Performance Poetry

Grade Prep - 3

Michelle Worthington

Copyright © 2024 Michelle Worthington
Copyright illustrations © Aya Suarjaya
Copyright illustrations © https://canva.com
Cover Art © Luke Harris Working Type Studio Australia

All rights reserved. No part of this publication may be reproduced, distributed, or transmitted in any form or by any means, without prior written permission.

Michelle Worthington/Daisy Lane Publishing
https://daisylanepublishing.com
https://michelleworthington.com

Publisher's Note: This is a work of fiction. Names, characters, places, and incidents are a product of the author's imagination. Locales and public names are sometimes used for atmospheric purposes. Any resemblance to actual people, living or dead, or to businesses, companies, events, institutions, or locales is completely coincidental.

Alien In My Pocket: Cosmic Characters For Performance Poetry
1st ed.

National Library of Australia Catalogue

ISBN 978-0-6458427-7-7 SC

ISBN 978-0-6458427-8-4 eBook

For Mrs Tremaine

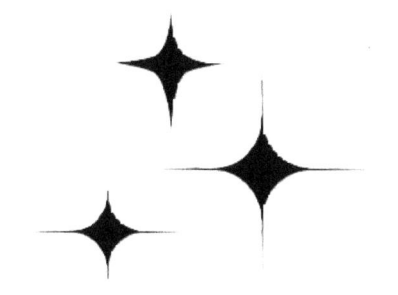

CONTENTS

There's An Alien In My Pocket 6
Bob The Brain Sucker 8
My Pet Alien 10
Aliens Love To Disco 13
The Quirk Of Quasars 15
Too Much Space 17
Heavenly Haiku 19
Spaceman 20
Stars 21
Space Race Haiku 22
Alien Talk 23
Alien Town 25
Space 27
Alien Lullaby 30
Alien 31
What To Do If You Meet An Alien 32
Purple Alien 35
I'm A Star 37
Alien Speak 39
Peanut The Alien 40
Alien Pizza 42

There's an Alien in My Pocket

In my pocket, oh so snug,

Lives an alien that looks like a bug.

With antennas wiggling, and eyes so wide,

It hopped in there to go for a ride.

Its skin is green, like a pickle jar,

With tiny toes in the shape of a star.

It giggles and squiggles, a jolly fellow,

In my pocket, which is turning yellow!

I asked, "How'd you end up in my shirt?"

It winked and said, "Hello there, squirt!

Your world is strange, but your pockets cozy,

I thought, 'Why not? I'm feeling dozy!'"

It speaks in beeps, in a language rare,

Says it's from a planet way out there.

But in my pocket, it feels just right,

Snug as a bug on a starry night.

So if you feel a tickle or a tiny cheer,

Maybe an alien is living near.

Check your pocket, you might just see,

A funny friend, happy as can be!

Bob The Brain Sucker

I am Bob, the brain sucking alien.
I am solid. I am stuck.
I am welded to your dome top
With my super alien suck.

I will creep along the waterline
Or blend in on wide open plains.
I am Bob, the brain sucking alien.
I am Ruler of the brains.

What do I care for the thing called biscuit
Or the donut with jam inside?
With my unrelenting sucker
And my sparkly underside.

There is only one thing I'm after
For those who try to prise at me.
And that's to watch their fingernails

As they go floating out to sea.

Don't upset me. I'm an alien.
And your brains I will devour.
There is only one problem I have.
I can only move an inch an hour!

So if you wouldn't mind waiting for me.
Please stop moving. And when you do,
If you could stand there for a fortnight
I will suck your brains out, too!

My Pet Alien

I found myself an alien

And I hoped in time he might

Become my friend and ward off

Things that go bump in the night.

I tried so hard to love him

And I didn't scream or shout

As he bit into the sofa

And dragged the stuffing out

I gave lots of goodies

But it was clear to see

That he ate things he found

Instead of things from me.

He ate my lovely carpet

He nibbled on the door

And when we wasn't chewing

He was weeing on the floor.

I bought a book on training

And read it all one night

And first thing in the morning

I thought we'd got it right.

Until he chomped the neighbour

And Nan's leg got a gnaw

Though I told him off, the message

Didn't seem to reach his jaw.

One day I drove him over

And I gave him to my friend

Who welcomed him and trained him

And got eaten. That's the end!

Alien's Love To Disco

Aliens love to disco

The music warms their soul

They dance in bare feet

And move to the beat

Till they turn as black as coal.

Aliens love to tango

They sway to the beat all day

Just give them a groove

And watch them all move

Till the DJ runs away.

You've never seen nothing like it.

They tear up the floor through the night.

When they salsa and spin

With an alien grin

Under the speckles of light.

The Quirks of Quasars

In the cosmic dance where stars hold sway,

Beyond the night, in the Milky Way,

There lies a tale of twinkling light,

A quasar's burst comes into sight.

The quirks of quasars, mysterious and bright,

Like cosmic beacons in the deep, black night,

They shimmer and they gleam, in a distant song,

A celestial waltz that's endlessly long.

A quasar's heart, a voracious maw,

Devouring matter, its cosmic law,

Yet in this chaos, a brilliance glows,

A paradox in the way it shows.

Billions of years, their light takes flight,

Across the universe, painting the night,

Through nebulae and starry streams,

A dance of brilliance, beyond our dreams.

Yet, what tales do quasars yearn to tell,

Of galaxies far, where do they dwell?

Do they whisper secrets of the ancient skies,

In the language of the cosmic ties?

Do they speak of worlds that we can't see,

Of wonders and realms where we could be?

In the quirks of quasars, there lies a lore,

A secret of the universe, forevermore.

Too Much Space

In the velvety depths of the cosmic tapestry

Where stars twinkle like a thousand mischievous eyes

There exists a wonderland far beyond the reaches of earthly imagination.

A cosmic dance floor, where planets waltz and comets pirouette

Nebulae shimmer in iridescent gowns of interstellar gas.

This is a realm where the ordinary rules of reality dissolve

And the extraordinary takes flight.

Meteors are cosmic fireflies

Lighting up the night as they streak across the sky

leaving trails of stardust in their wake.

Planets, adorned in rings of ice and dust, spin like galactic ballerinas

Performing an eternal ballet choreographed by the hand of gravity.

Nebulae are celestial artists painting the sky with hues of pink, purple, and electric blue.

They are the creators of stars, sculpting them from vast clouds of gas and dust

Stellar nurseries where new suns and planets come to life.

The black holes are enigmatic portals to the unknown

They are the cosmic storytellers, whispering tales of galaxies devoured and spacetime bent

Inviting us to ponder the mysteries of the universe.

Every star is a lighthouse, guiding the way for dreamers, poets, and explorers.

It's a place where the imagination takes flight on wings of stardust

The boundaries of reality blur into a realm of infinite possibilities.

Let your mind wander among the constellations

Let the whimsy of the cosmos inspire your dreams

In space, the extraordinary becomes the everyday

And the ordinary transforms into the extraordinary.

Heavenly Haiku

Silver saucers glide,

Extraterrestrial eyes,

Stars whisper their tale.

Spaceman

Starry night above,

Planets dance, moon whispers dreams,

Space adventure calls.

Stars

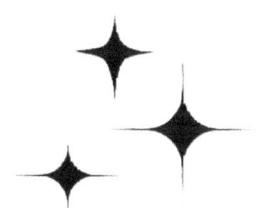

Twinkle in the night,

Stars play hide-and-seek with the

Moon, a sparkling light.

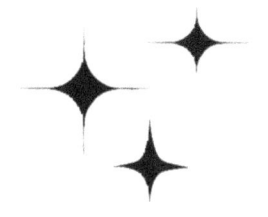

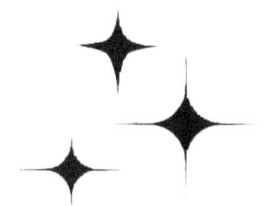

Space Race Haiku

Rocket in the sky,

Zooming way up, oh so high,

Adventure nearby.

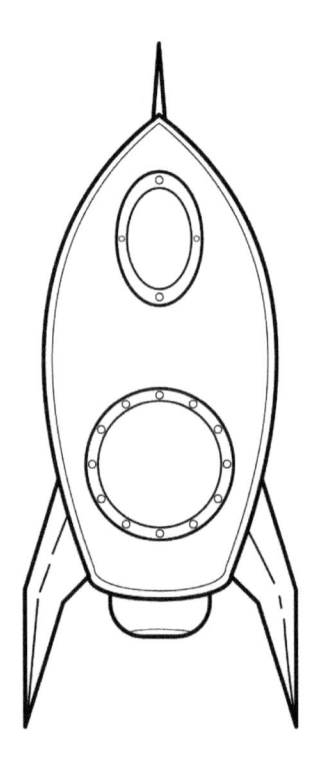

Alien Talk

Zap, zoom, in the cosmic gloom,
Aliens land with a sonic boom.
Whirr and chirp, their language unique,
In the galactic dance, a rhythm they seek.

Gleaming saucers, beep and hum,
In the stellar playground, a cosmic strum.
Ping, pong, echoes in the night,
As aliens giggle in the starlight.

Twinkle, sparkle, their eyes aglow,
A cosmic lullaby, a celestial show.
Buzz and bop, a dance so rare,
Aliens shimmy through the cosmic air.

Crackle, pop, their laughter rings,
In the space-time symphony, they sing.
Swoosh and swirl, in an alien trance,
Their otherworldly moves, a stellar dance.

Whoosh, whisper, secrets unfold,
In the intergalactic story, so bold.
Snap, crackle, in the astral sea,
Aliens and their dancing spree.

Tick, tock, the cosmic clock,
As aliens frolic on a moonlit dock.
Beep, bloop, a cosmic delight,
In the language of aliens, pure and bright.

Alien Town

In Alientown,

where peculiar happenings were as common as morning coffee,

an inventor of delightful drinks

accidentally spilled a cup of his latest concoction on his beloved cat,

Mr. Whiskerstein.

Instead of the anticipated fizzy reaction,

a mysterious whooshing sound filled the air,

and both inventor and cat

vanished into the cosmic unknown.

Fish sailed through the skies

like intergalactic acrobats.

Together, they devised a plan

involving homemade gadgets and a sprinkle of glitter—

because, as the cat

who could now talk

 insisted,

"Every adventure needs a touch of sparkle!"

The inventor activated the device

and the cat said

"brace for weirdness"

holding a contraption made of kitchen utensils

and glittery pipe cleaners.

With their glitter-powered gadgetry,

the inventor pulled himself

and his floating talking cat

back into Alientown,

narrowly avoiding smacking into a flying fish.

As the portal closed, the inventor grinned and remarked,

"Well, that was an out-of-this-world experience!

Who knew interdimensional travel could be so... uplifting?"

while his cat sailed around the room

singing songs about space.

Space

Vast

Endless

Cosmic

Silent.

Glowing

Stars

Whisper

Secrets.

Nebulas

Dance

Galaxies

Spiral.

Mysteries

Unfold

Beyond

Time.

Black

Holes

Swallow

Light.

Celestial

Bodies

Orbit

Spin.

Eternal

Void

Awaits

Exploration.

Infinite

Possibilities

Unveiled

Space.

Alien Lullaby

Close your little eyes, it's time for night,

In the cradle of the moon's soft light.

The world is quiet, stars are in the sky,

Aliens are watching as you close your eyes.

The night is filled with whispers, a lullaby so clear,

Aliens are whispering in your ear.

The aliens are watching, they are not asleep,

As you fall into a dream world deep.

Hush-a-bye, in your cozy bed,

As aliens try to invade your head.

Dream of hiding places, under the moon,

Hush-a-bye, my baby, aliens will come soon.

Alien

A nother

L anding

E scaping

I nternational

N otice

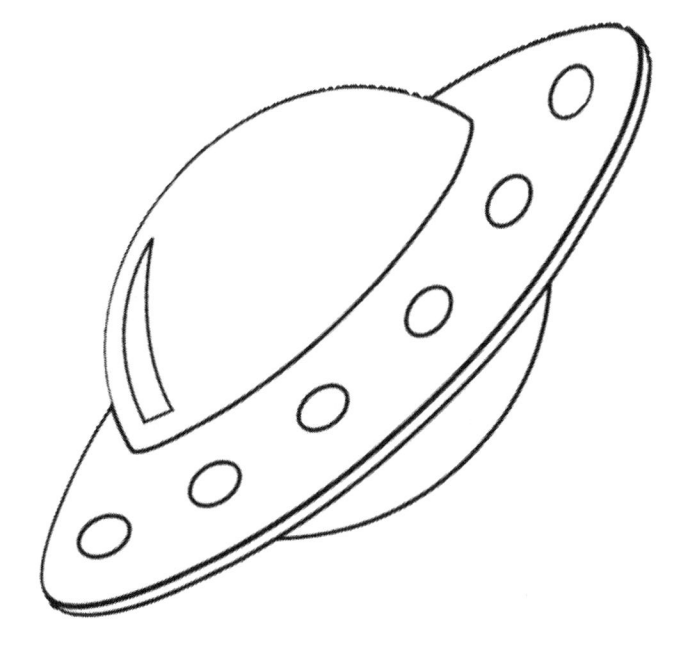

What To Do If You Meet An Alien

From a world beyond our own,

where the sky wears a glittery gown

and planets throw a celestial party,

imagine you stumble upon a fuzzy, green, three-eyed alien.

First, don't panic!

Aliens love laughter,

so start with a funny face

and a goofy dance.

If that doesn't work,

offer a handshake

with your left foot.

Next, share your favorite Earth snack.

Aliens are crazy about crunchy things,

so hand over your crispiest potato chips

or the loudest popcorn you can find.

All aliens adore music.

Sing them a tune,

even if it's just "Twinkle, Twinkle, Little Star"

Throw in some alien dance moves

wobble like a jellyfish

or hop like a moon bunny.

Remember, if it pulls out a space-age gadget,

don't mistake it for a something scary.

Ask politely,

"Is that a teleporting toaster

or a sandwich squisher?"

Aliens appreciate honesty.

Lastly, gift them a souvenir from Earth,

like a shiny pebble

or a rubber ducky.

They collect odd treasures from every planet they visit.

So, if you ever cross paths with an alien,

just be yourself,

share a laugh,

dance like nobody's watching,

and create an out-of-this-world friendship that's simply stellar!

Purple Alien

Purple Alien

From the sun,

Come with me

And have some fun.

You do your dance

And I will sing

On the planet

Where you are King.

There is no castle.

There is no gold.

There is no dragon

Or knights of old.

In your kingdom
Above the stars
Somewhere between
Venus and Mars.

Your gold is laughter
Your silver is smiles
Your conga line
Stretches for miles.

Your people are safe
With lots of food
And everyone's happy
And in a good mood.
Purple Alien
From Outer Space
I wish you could teach
The Human Race.

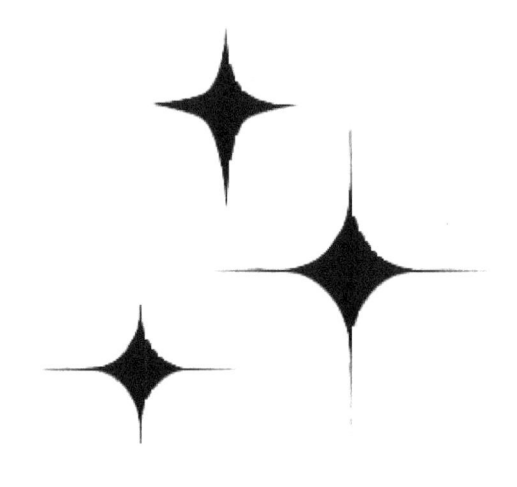

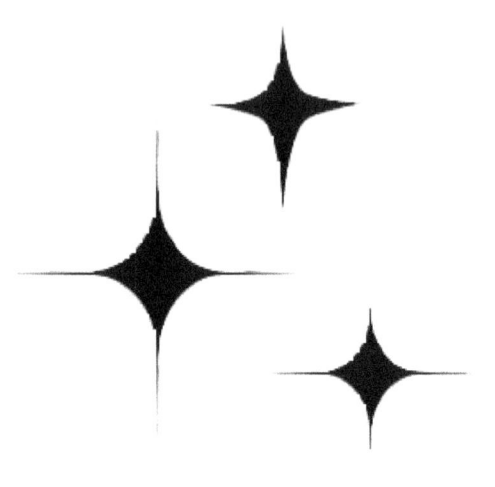

I'm A Star

I'm a star

Twinkling bright

Shining in the

Sky at night

I'm a star

I'm burning hot

I shimmer down

With all I've got

I'm a star

Watch me glow

My light has got

So far to go.

I'm a star

Twinkling bright

Wave to me

In the sky tonight.

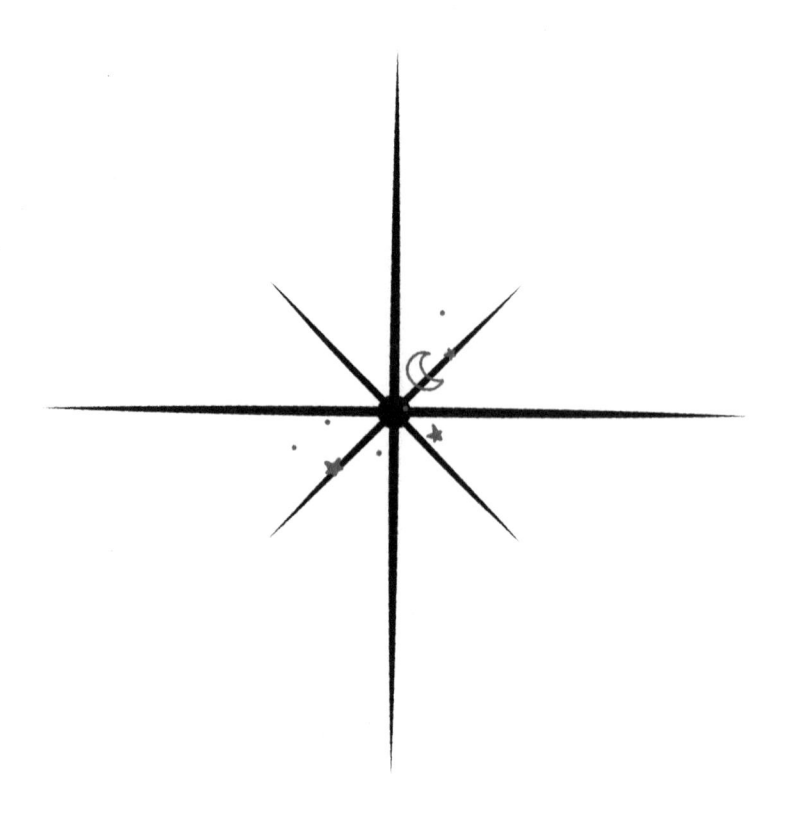

Alien Speak

Beep

Snarkle spitty loop

Boop

Digle dagle doop

Pong

Obb Gig Puggle

Ping

Sint da muddle

Glop

Fram getto flub

Glip

Dharm specko drub

Peanut The Alien

My name is Peanut

I'm a Zog

I was born

On the planet Gog

My skin is green

My hair is blue

My eyes are red

My feet are too.

They call me Peanut

Beause I'm small

But I am smart

I beat them all

I have a brain

That likes to feed

So lots of books

Are what I need

I feed my brain

With things I've read

Because my mouth

Is on my head!

Alien Pizza

Moon cheese gleams bright,

Saucer spins in cosmic flight,

Aliens crave every bight.

Aliens love pizza!

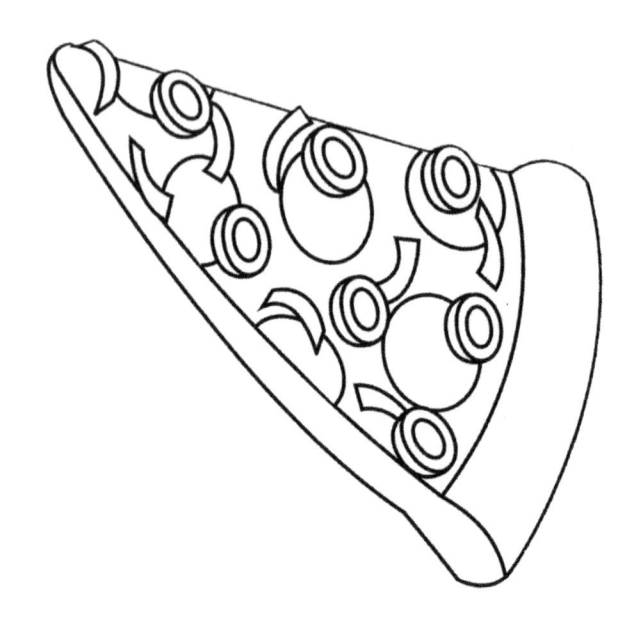

International award winning author, scriptwriter and actress. A full-time writer based in Brisbane, Michelle credits her three sons for giving her an endless source of inspiration, as well as her wrinkles.

Two-time winner of the International Book Award, Michelle has twice been short listed for a CBCA Picture Book of the Year Award and Australian Speech Pathology Award. Michelle was the recipient of the 2018 AusMumpreneur Gold Award for Business Excellence and the winner of the 2018 Redlands BaR award for Best Start Up Business. Her scripts have been finalists at the California Women's Film Festival, Kids First Film Festival, Gold Coast International Film Festival and 4th Dimenson International Indie Film Festival. In 2021, she won the AFIN International Film Award for Best Screenplay. In 2023, she won the Best Unproduced Screenplay Award at the New York International Film Festival.

Michelle is dedicated to encouraging a strong love of reading and writing in young children and enjoys working with charities that support the vision of empowering youth through education. As a mentor and editor, she helps aspiring authors find pathways to publication and enjoys working as part of a team in projects that are purposeful, innovative and inspirational.